RADSPORTS GUIDES

FREESTYLE MOTO-X

TRACY NELSON MAURER

Rourke Publishing LLC
Vero Beach, Florida 32964

www.rourkepublishing.com

Project Assistance:
Bobby "Rage" LePage, Duluth, MN, signed on with Polaris in 2001 at 16 years of age. A Sno-Cross champion and FMX/MX rider, he runs anything with a motor—fast. Rick Halvorson rode MX competitions through the 1970s and now shares his enthusiasm for the sport with his son Sean.

Also, the author extends appreciation to Mike Maurer, Kendall and Lois M. Nelson, Harlan Maurer, and Drs. Steven Massopust, Timothy Rich, and Boyd Erdman.

Photo Credits:
Pages 4, 34, 36, 37, 41: © Al Bello/Allsport; Pages 7, 16, 20: © Jon Ferrey/Allsport; Pages 7, 8, 23, 26: © Gregory Gage/American Racing Journal; Page 31: © David Leeds/Allsport; Page 33: © Jed Jacobsohn/Allsport; Pages 35, 43: © David Leeds/Allsport

Editorial Services:
Pamela Schroeder

Notice: This book contains information that is true, complete, and accurate to the best of our knowledge. However, the author and Rourke Publishing LLC offer all recommendations and suggestions without any guarantees and disclaim all liability incurred in connection with the use of this information.

Safety first! Activities appearing or described in this publication may be dangerous. Always wear safety gear. Even with complete safety gear, risk of injury still exists.

Library of Congress Cataloging-in-Publication Data

Maurer, Tracy Nelson.
  Freestyle Moto - X / Tracy Nelson Maurer
    p. cm — (Radsports guides)
  Includes bibliographical references and index.
  Summary: Surveys the history, equipment, techniques, and safety factors of freestyle off-road
    motorcycle racing.
  ISBN 1-58952-101-3
    1. Motocross—Juvenile literature. [1. Motocross.]I. Title.

GV1060.12 .M38 2001
796.7'56—dc21   2001041654

Printed in the USA

TABLE OF CONTENTS

FMX riders try to catch big air off killer jumps. They fly 50 feet (15.2 m) into the air and pull daring moves like this.

POWERFUL FUN

Freestyle Motocross, or FMX, pushes power, tricks, fun and danger to the limit. The kinds of moves you see on bicycles or skateboards now come in a hard-core and amped-up motorized version. This intense style of motorcycle riding grew from motocross, or off-road motorcycle racing—also a gnarly sport.

Motocross traces its roots to Europe in the 1920s. Dusty races, called scrambles, tested motorcycle riders' skills on rough **terrain**. They rode mostly unpaved roads, but the real challenge came from holding on at top-end speeds quivering near 50 mph (80 kph). Your first minibike probably would have dusted them.

chapter

ONE

MX MAKES ITS MARK

Sometime in the 1950s, motocross began appearing as Moto-X or MX. The sport found a new home among Americans then. Who else loves motors, especially racing engines, better? Still, motocross stalled out a few times between then and now.

Surfers and mountain snowboarders, already big into tricks, latched onto the sport in the early 1990s. Motocross became a favorite cross-training sport for them because it builds strength, balance, and **endurance**. It's also never boring.

TUNE IN FROM HOME

Today MX rips across television screens almost every weekend. Tune in and you'll see 40 riders bust out at the start, jostling to break ahead. A few crash and the pack thins out. They churn and skid through curves, looking for the fastest line. Rear wheels spit rocks and mud as the bikes slide and chew up the hills. Riders fly off jumps and blitz **whoop-de-dos**, a nasty series of small, tightly spaced bumps.

Sometimes they reach 80 miles (129 km) per hour. But controlling the bikes through the rutted dirt can mean dropping down to 30 miles (48 km) per hour. Up, down, and around they ride, usually 20 times around a 1 1/4 mile (2 km) lap before passing the checkered flag.

Moto-X racing is extremely aggressive and wiping out can be hazardous.

7

Riding over whoops in a championship race.

WHOOPING IT UP

Look closely at how a serious rider attacks whoop-de-doos.

1. He shifts his weight to the rear of the bike and bends his knees. Leaning forward nose dives the front wheel into the gully.

2. He tries to stay on top of the bumps by coming into them with speed and **momentum**, often in fourth gear.

For long and widely spaced whoops, you need a different **strategy**, especially on a small bike. The rider takes them like a rhythm section, bouncing off the seat but keeping his weight neutral.

Some pros practice doing wheelies, or riding on the back wheel, over flat ground to gain control and balance.

RAD TIP

Wheelie Wizards: The first riders attempting to set the world record for wheelies covered more than 100 miles (160 km) before they plopped back down onto two wheels. They didn't lose their balance. They ran out of gas. In 1991, a Japanese motorcyclist rode a wheelie for 205.7 miles (329.12 km) to set a new record.

SUPERCROSS AMPS UP THE ACTION

Supercross, or SMX, blends some traditional motocross racing with a bit of freestyle jumping. Unlike the natural outdoor courses of motocross races, Supercross features man-made dirt tracks in indoor and outdoor stadiums. Different obstacles, including jumps and spine or T-ramps, challenge the riders.

The SMX circuit requires that riders turn 16 years of age before trying to qualify. Most riders drop out when the riding becomes this serious. Like professional football and other big-league sports, SMX sees only the best of the best at this level.

Watching MX or SMX at home yanks you onto the edge of your seat. But if you're lucky, you catch the whiff of fresh exhaust fumes up close. Even better, you learn to ride motocross.

RAD TIP

Pros Plan Ahead
Pros check out the MX course before they ride. They try to picture their lines on the banked curves, or berms.

Supercross takes the sport to a whole new level.

RIDERS RIDE, RIDE, RIDE

Motocross riders, boys and girls, start as young as seven on flat tracks, or simple dirt courses. Age and size matter less than fitness. On top of steel nerves, you need sturdy balance, plus strong and flexible muscles—especially if you try tricks. One of motorcycling's most grueling races, MX also demands mental **stamina**. Daydream on the course and you'll see stars (and maybe the medical team) in seconds.

A cocky attitude holds you back, too. Posers, or riders who act like they know MX but really don't know a pastrami from a Pastrana, eat a lot of dirt. Ask experienced riders questions. Join a motocross club and practice with better riders. Read books and surf the Internet. You fast-track your skills that way.

Ride, ride, and ride some more. Practice makes you better. The bike doesn't win the race. You do.

GEARING UP FOR MX

You need a bike to ride, of course. Motocross bikes use thick, knobby tires to grip the dirt tracks. Large **shock absorbers** and springs on these bikes help smooth out your ride.

Don't plan to spend time cruising the city streets. Motocross bikes do not meet the legal codes for street riding. You'd face a stiff fine for breaking the law.

Motocross bikes mainly use three engine sizes, measured in cubic centimeters (cc): 125cc, 250cc, or 500cc. Sports centers and motorcycle shops sell other sizes, too. Engine size sets the race classes. You always race against riders on the same size bike.

chapter

TWO

BIKE BASICS

Depending on your size, skill, and style of riding, you may like a bigger or smaller bike. The heavier 500cc bikes launch like rockets. They also lack some control on jumps and curves.

The 250cc bikes handle bumps and turns well and still deliver decent speed. Supercross and motocross racers ride 250cc bikes.

Many young motocross riders stay with the lighter 125cc bikes. These bikes also work best for tricks.

YOUR FIRST CAUTION FLAG

This flag isn't yellow; it's green—as in green dollar signs. Prepare yourself and your parents for the costs ahead. A basic 125cc bike runs from $4,500 to $5,500. A 250cc bike starts around $5,500.

Check the newspaper and motorcycle shops for used bikes. You might find a deal. If you buy used, check for engine wear. Motocross pistons and rings take a beating.

Maintenance is the best way to make your money go further. Clean your machine after every ride. Hose off the mud. Dry it and polish it.

Invest in a good set of tools now and you'll save on shop service fees later. Learn to make your own adjustments. Do some light bedtime reading and study the owner's manual. All kinds of tips hide in that little book. Find them. Memorize the maintenance check list.

RAD TIP

Baby That Baby
Make a copy of the routine maintenance check list in the manual. Post it in your garage as a reminder. Mark when you check the engine fluids, tires, and other bike parts. A maintenance record comes in handy when your bike visits the repair shop or when you sell it.

Check out the different bike sizes in your nearest showroom.

*The bike is just one expense. You also need
protective gear, including a full-face helmet or lid.*

STOCK MACHINERY

The dealers say you can ride your motocross bike right out the showroom door. Stock bikes, or machines without any **retrofits**, can tear up the track just fine, thank you very much.

Flip through a motorcycle magazine or surf an on line shopping site, and you'll find all kinds of do-dads to add. Some riders add protective shields around the handlebars. This protects their hands, but it also keeps the throttles and clutches from shoveling dirt. The most common product for motocross bikes is stickers—and lots of them.

BUT WAIT, THERE'S MORE!

Oh, you're not done spending the big bucks—not even close! Riders wear special clothing and safety gear. Start at the top with a full-faced helmet. Nobody with a brain rides without a lid. Competitions require safety-certified helmets. Goggles, padded gloves, and motocross pants also up your protection level.

Most riders wear body **armor**, too. This lightweight, vented shield has a hard plastic shell with foam rubber inside to cushion your crashes. It fits snugly on your chest and back with wings over the shoulders.

Sturdy leather boots with steel tips handle the dabs, or toe touches, you make on tight turns. Some men and women wear them in public, too. (No comment from the fashion police.)

Now throw in travel costs, bike maintenance, and hauling your bike around. Don't forget the time you spend, too. You put in hours and hours and hours practicing, cleaning your bike, washing your gear, and planning your race.

Is it worth it? Hoo-yah, speed freak.

WARM UP YOUR ENGINE

Motocross racing or freestyle motocross beats on your body. Pros work out on rowing machines. They follow a strict routine with freeweights and stretching. Many cross-train on BMX (bicycles) or mountain bikes. Toned muscles improve performance and recover from injuries better.

Before you hop onto your bike, take 5 minutes to warm up. Start with 20 or 30 jumping jacks. Then do at least 15 push ups. Once your heart rate is up, stretch out. Sit on the ground and reach for your toes with a flat back. Hold the stretch for 20 seconds.

Standing up, use your left hand to pull your right elbow across your chest. Hold it for 20 seconds. Switch elbows.

Then step out and lunge at the same time. Your lower knee should almost touch the floor while the other one is square to it. Switch back and forth, from one leg to the other, about 15 times. This stretches your inner thighs.

Most motocross riders train for their sport. Mountain biking is perfect for building strength in your legs.

Ride only in areas set aside for motocross.

BRRAAAAAAAAAAAAAP

Nothing sounds quite like MX bikes roaring down a trail. Loud and noisy, motocross bikes also tear up the natural landscape. A lot of places won't roll out the welcome mat for you.

Some states even try to ban kids 16 and under from riding at all—even as passengers on touring bikes with parents driving! Check the American Motorcycle Association's website for the latest legal battles.

What's the best way to keep MX legal? Ride only in areas set aside for bikes. A local club or motocross dealer can point you in the right direction.

RAD TIP

Push Some Air
Engine power delivers speed. Your bike goes faster when you push it harder. What holds you back? The bike's weight and drag from the tires kissing pavement slow you down until you reach 30 miles (48 km) per hour. Then it's air. By 100 miles (160 km) per hour, you burn about 89 percent of your engine power just pushing air.

BEEN THERE, BROKE THAT

Riders collect an amazing variety of injuries even dressed in full armor. Hips and elbows often suffer from road rash, or light scrapes and cuts. Most road rash looks gross, but it's not serious.

Wash the dirt, gravel, or glass out as soon as you can. Put on **antiseptic** cream or spray, and let it scab over. If the scab dries hard and cracks, soften it with a thin layer of **petroleum** jelly.

Most road rash doesn't need gauze unless it's from your first wipe out of the day and you know you'll get it full of dirt again. However, you might want to cover it in public. Why needlessly gross out your parents or other admirers?

HOSPITAL HUSTLE

See a doctor if the road rash won't come clean. If the scrape looks deep and meaty, don't mess around—go to the doctor. Untreated wounds can become infected.

Knocking your noggin around in your helmet may make you see stars. Sit down and put your head between your knees. If your vision stays cloudy or if you feel stabbing pains anywhere, ask someone to bring you to the doctor right away.

Broken legs, torn spleens, cracked skulls, and other major body damage pull you off your bike for awhile. Do what the doctor says so you heal faster. Some pros even work out in their wheelchairs.

Ouch! Hopefully the rider's protective gear took most of the beating.

DON'T GO DOWN WITH THE SHIP

Wipe outs happen. Some days they happen on every run. Bailing, or ditching your bike before it crashes, can save you from hospital time.

You don't want to go down with the ship. Staying on your bike in a crash is like dancing with a flying chainsaw. The heat and moving parts chew you up. The weight of the machine can kill you.

The moment you lose control, push the machine away from you and jump in the other direction. Roll out and away from the bike. Don't try to flatten it out or save it from wrecking. You can replace a bike. You, however, are a one-shot deal.

DAREDEVILS & DUDES

Evel Knievel amazed the world with his daring jumps back in the 1970s. Those early flights almost seem tame compared to today's motorcycle jumping and FMX airborne action.

Jumpers like Evel's son Robbie Knievel and showman Seth Enslow look for distance. They don't do many tricks. Doug Danger set the world record at 251 feet (76.55 m) years ago, and Seth and others want to shatter it. They practice jumping over Harley-Davidsons, semi-trucks, and kegs of beer at events like the Free Air Festival of Freestyle Motocross.

chapter
THREE

Shift your weight to the rear of the bike and keep the front wheel up. To nail the perfect landing the rear wheel has to touch down first.

NAIL THE LANDING

Jumping isn't nearly as hard as landing. Bikes often leave the take off ramp at more than 55-60 mph (88-96 km/h). The rider holds the front wheel up in the air and keeps the rear wheel turning. The rear wheel touches down on the landing ramp first. If it's not spinning, it skids.

Ramp angle, bike control, and take off speed affect where the rider lands. Too much speed and the rider overshoots his target. Seth Enslow cruised 245 feet (74.7 m) practicing his jumps in April, 2001, but overshot his mark. A double skull fracture, crushed eye socket, and more than 50 stitches sidelined the dude for awhile.

Pro stunt riders also jump through panes of glass or walls of fire. Safety comes first. They wear special clothing and **modify** their bikes for the trick. In fire jumping, an ordinary engine would starve for oxygen and die.

RAD TIP

Newton Knew It
Sir Isaac Newton discovered **"gyroscopic force"** and you still use it today when you ride a bike or motorcycle. He knew a body moving in circular motion tends to hold its position. So a motorcycle stays up as long as the wheels spin. May the force be with you.

REVVING UP A NEW SPORT

Many of today's top FMX pros, sometimes called pilots, began in motocross. But they had more fun nailing tricks at the back of the pack than speeding for the checkered flag. The media started calling them free-riders in the early 1990s. Still called free-riders or FMX riders, they create new tricks all the time.

FMX shares a history with BMX (bicycle motocross) tricks. Many pros still practice on BMX bikes before they try tricks on motorcycles.

chapter
FOUR

FROM WHIPS TO FLIPS

One of the first tricks motocross racers learn is the whip. They push their bikes sideways to the landing in the air and straighten up in time for the landing. Wheelies, with the front wheel in the air, and a Bucking Bronco, with the back wheel in the air, look easy. They're not. Like all tricks, they take a lot of practice.

Carey Hart, famous for ripping the first back flip, tried the flip over and over again on a BMX bike. He practiced at a special camp with mats to cushion his falls. Everyone thought he was crazy, even other riders. They still do.

FMX tricks promise to stay wild, too. FMX took to the snow recently. Jumping on dirt just wasn't enough.

Busting big-air tricks challenges most people. Start with something simple like the whip or a wheelie.

HANG ON, THIS FUN'S JUST BEGUN

Still a young sport, FMX riders claim new sick, or awesome, tricks all the time. They raise the standards for everyone else. Pilots name their tricks, making for some unusual titles out there. FMX also uses its own language. It borrows from BMX, skateboarding, and other edge sports. Check the Internet for the latest lingo.

Remember, only advanced riders should try FMX tricks.

Based on a scale of 1 (easiest) to 10 (hardest),
here are a few faves:

#1

5.0 Difficulty
No Footer

While in the air, the rider kicks both feet off the foot pegs and balances on the seat. Taking their hands off the handlebars at the same time adds two points of difficulty. Riders often combine tricks for extra style points. After a big-air move like a Superman, riders might finish with a No-Hander Lander—taking their hands off the handlebars when they land.

Many FMX tricks began as BMX (bicycle) tricks. Here, a rider prepares to pull a *Suicide, a No-Hander-Lander with his hands behind his back.*

Riders often add a Heel Clicker on other moves for extra style.

#2
7.0 Difficulty
Heel Clicker

With his hands on the grips, the rider brings his feet over the handlebars and clicks his heels together over the front fender. Add the Heel Clicker onto other tricks for extra style points.

With the Bar Hop, the rider tries to stretch his feet out over the fender.

#3
8.0 Difficulty
Bar Hop

The rider shoots his legs through his arms and holds them above the handlebars. Extra style points for reaching the feet out over the fender.

A Superman Seat Grab challenges advanced riders. Carey Hart invented a variation called the Hart Attack.

#4

9.0 Difficulty
Superman Seat Grab With Indian Leg Whip

Holding onto the grips, the rider lays his legs out backwards and even with the seat. Then he releases one hand and grabs the seat as he pulls a huge scissors kick with his legs. He gets extra points for full extension. Another variation of the Superman, the Hart Attack takes the rider's legs straight up in the air like a handstand. Carey Hart invented this off-the-chart move.

The Lazy Boy looks relaxing but it takes intense concentration to balance the bike this way.

#5

9.0 Difficulty
Lazy Boy

The rider stretches his legs out in front of the bike under the handlebars. He lies back on the seat as far as possible with his hands over his head. Extra style points for stretching way out.

OFF THE CHART

The Back Flip and double-rider tricks rank off the charts. One of the most amazing double-rider tricks combines the Lazy Boy and the Bar Hop. The first bike launches off the ramp closely followed by the second bike. The first rider pulls the Lazy Boy, reaching out his hands so far that he touches the second rider's foot in the Bar Hop. Now that's sick.

FMX NAMES ITS CHAMPS

Televised competitions kicked FMX into high gear. The sport exploded onto the "extreme" scene in 1998. The International Freestyle Motocross Association (IFMA) began that same year. The first IFMA-sanctioned series followed in 1999, headed by the Vans Triple Crown.

Still hosted annually, riders earn points for each event. At the end of the series, the rider with the most points takes home the championship.

chapter
FIVE

Another venture begun in the late 1990s, the LXD's FreeRide Motocross also challenges pilots to fly higher and perform bolder tricks. These shows draw huge crowds.

JUDGED SHOWS

Free-riders roar onto a dirt track, about 200 feet (60 m) square. Dump trucks bring in thousands of yards (meters) of dirt to shape the terrain. Bulldozers and old-fashioned shovels sculpt massive gap jumps, ramp-to-ramp **transitions**, and plenty of obstacles.

Some competitions use metal ramps with dirt landings. Many riders prefer metal ramps because the surfaces don't rut out like dirt. Pilots know what to expect every time they hit the ramps. The perfect angle pushes them higher in the air, too.

Riders pick their lines and pull their tricks. Judges award points for air height, creativity, and style. Unlike racing, where one person clearly finishes first, FXM bows to the judges' decisions.

Tricks like this one push the sport to the edge.

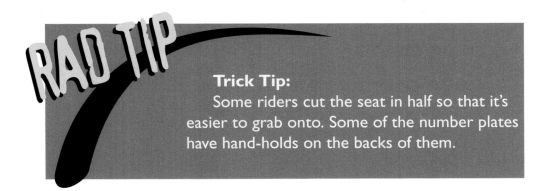

RAD TIP

Trick Tip:
Some riders cut the seat in half so that it's easier to grab onto. Some of the number plates have hand-holds on the backs of them.

BIG-TIME INVITATION

The IFMA invites any experienced rider to qualify for the big-time pro shows. You must complete an application and send a video of your tricks with a racing or freestyle **résumé**, plus your parents' permission if you're under 18 years of age.

Even if the IFMA invites you to an event, you still have to qualify during the day. Then you can ride in the show that night. The IFMA **automatically** counts you as a member when you qualify and you pay no fees.

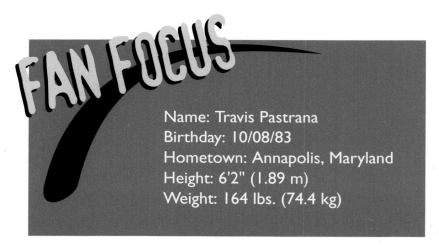

FAN FOCUS

Name: Travis Pastrana
Birthday: 10/08/83
Hometown: Annapolis, Maryland
Height: 6'2" (1.89 m)
Weight: 164 lbs. (74.4 kg)

Travis won his first motorcycling competition at age five. The trophy towered over him. Travis kept on winning both motocross races and freestyle contests. At 16—the first year he was eligible for Supercross—he became the first person to win the professional 125cc National East Coast Championship in his rookie year.

Travis graduated from high school two years early and takes college courses via the Internet while he travels. He trains daily and works hard to push the sport to new levels.

Travis Pastrana gets big air during an X Games competition.

WILD FANS

FMX audiences rival WWF wrestling fans for volume and loyalty. However, FMX fans know the only thing fake about these riders might be some front teeth. Every ride defies gravity. Every jump could turn ugly with the smallest error. Fans know that the rock-hard ground forgives no mistakes.

Audiences scream and cheer for each trick, even for a few dead sailors (jumps without tricks). They try to win passes to the "pit parties" for autograph sessions.

Crowds of 33,000 easily pack stadiums to watch FMX and Super Moto-X. The huge fan support surprised many factory **executives**. They thought FMX was a fad. Suddenly, they scrambled to sign riders. The purses, or cash prizes, at competitions have grown, too.

Now you can check out the latest FMX action on sizzling videos, DVD, and even on computer games. Motocross has always **veered** off the beaten path. Get ready for the ride of your life!

FURTHER READING

Your library and the Internet can help you learn more about freestyle motocross. Check these titles and sites for starters:

Armentrout, David. *Motocross*. Vero Beach, Rourke Publishing LLC, 1997.

Guinness World Records 2001. London: Guinness World Records, 2000.

WEBSITES TO VISIT

www.ama-cycle.org

www.goodtimeswithcareyhart.com

www.expn.com

www.ExtremeSports.com

www.gravitygames.com

www.pacefmx.com

www.nofear.com

www.ronronmx.com

www.transworldmotocross.com

www.thefamilie.com

www.vans.com

GLOSSARY

antiseptic (an tih SEP tik) — a lotion, cream, or spray that kills germs

armor (AHR mur) — pads and other safety equipment

automatically (AW toh MAT ih klee) — done by itself

endurance (en DUHR ans) — ability to keep going

executives (ig ZEK yeh tivz) — business leaders

gyroscopic force (JY reh skahp ik   FORS) — a principle of movement
   that says spinning wheels will stay upright until they stop spinning

maintenance (MAYN teh nens) — cleaning, fixing, and caring
   for equipment

modify (MAHD uh fy) — to change

momentum (moh MEN tum) — forward or ongoing movement

petroleum (peh TROH lee um) — oil-based

résumé (REZ oo may) — an outline of past experiences, skills, and awards

retrofits (RET row fits) — equipment that replaces the originals

shock absorbers (SHAHK ub ZORB urz) — equipment that takes up jolts and bumps for a smoother ride

stamina (STAM eh nuh) — ability to keep going

strategy (STRAT eh jee) — plan

terrain (tuh RAYN)— ground or surface; landscape

transitions (trans ISH unz) — the curve of a ramp; or the connecting parts or space between two things, such as two ramps

veered (VEERD) — leaned or turned

whoop-de-dos (HWOOP dee DOOZ) — a series of tightly spaced bumps; also called whoops

INDEX

ABOUT THE AUTHOR

Tracy Nelson Maurer specializes in nonfiction and business writing. Her most recently published children's books include the *A to Z* series, also from Rourke Publishing LLC. She lives with her husband Mike and two children in Superior, Wisconsin.